You Can Draw M...

Introduction

This book is all about monsters! It's all about how to create them, draw and paint them. There are step-by-step drawings to help you and projects to do in a sketchbook. (Look out for the special sketchbook symbol below.) There are tips and advice on how to make your monsters scary, funny, friendly or fierce. But don't forget that the most important thing is to enjoy drawing.

Keeping a sketchbook

It's very important to keep a sketchbook. Always carry it with you so you can draw things you notice in the world around you and make written notes.

You can buy a sketchbook or make one by clipping pieces of paper together. It is a good idea to prepare the pages. Paint or stain each double page with a background wash of ink or watercolour. You can also line it with other paper, like brown paper or wallpaper. Look at the examples below. Make notes on how different drawing tools, pencil, pen, crayon or paint, respond to each surface.

wallpaper — brown paper — patches of colour (not too bright) — packaging and magazines partly covered with white — maps — lining paper — tissue — newspaper

Real-life Monsters

There is no substitute for looking at the real thing and trying to draw it. But you cannot very well go out and ask a monster to pose for you. However, you *can* draw real creatures that sometimes seem scary, like spiders, snakes, beetles and bats. This will be very useful when you are making up imaginary monsters.

Spiders

House spiders look fearsome but are, in fact, completely harmless. Catch them gently in a glass or jar. Draw them and then release them.

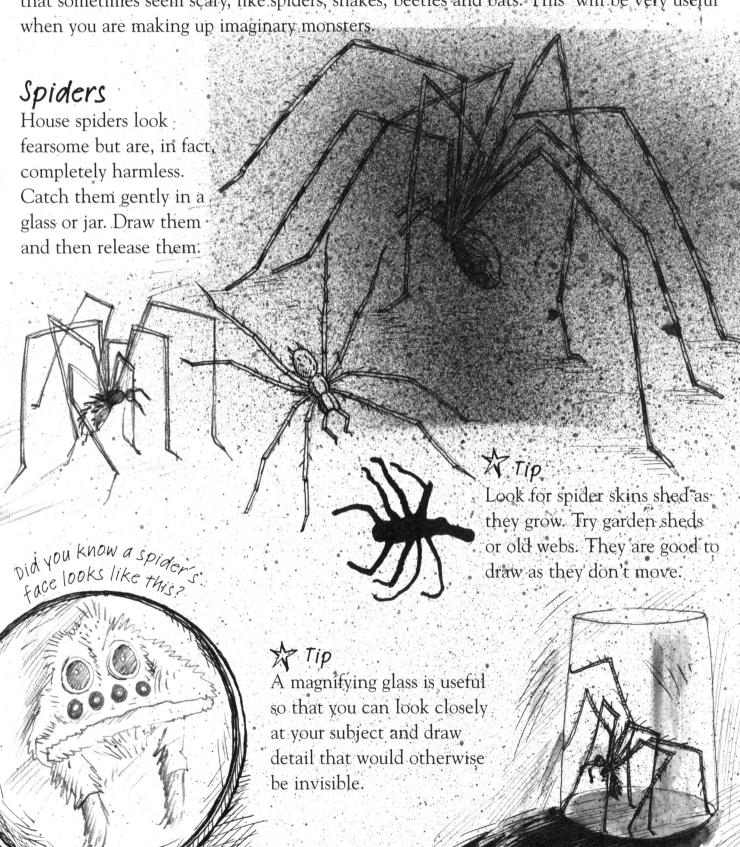

Did you know a spider's face looks like this?

☆ Tip
Look for spider skins shed as they grow. Try garden sheds or old webs. They are good to draw as they don't move.

☆ Tip
A magnifying glass is useful so that you can look closely at your subject and draw detail that would otherwise be invisible.

Stag beetles

These magnificent, harmless insects look like miniature aliens. Don't miss a chance to draw a live one or you might find a specimen in a museum.

 ## Key point

Always make several drawings from different viewpoints, not just one.

Drawing tool

A dip pen makes an exciting line. You could also use a sharpened feather.

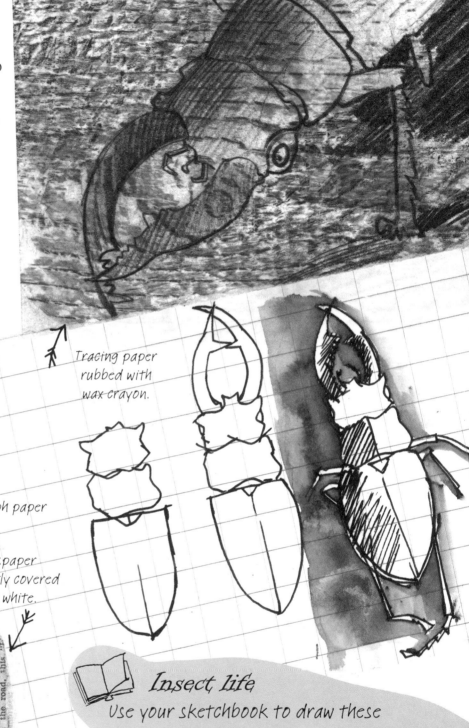

Tracing paper rubbed with wax crayon.

Graph paper

Newspaper partly covered with white.

Insect life

Use your sketchbook to draw these creatures. This will help you understand how they move and what it is about them that is scary. It will be very useful when you are making up imaginary monsters. Prepare your sketchbook with different surfaces (see page 1). Make notes as well as drawings. Note their size and colour, how shiny they are and so on.

Dinosaurs

These terrifying-looking beasts are another kind of real-life monster.

👁 Observe

You can gradually build your drawing up from two different-sized ovals. Notice its small arms. No-one really knows what purpose they served.

Tyrannosaurus rex

Shape

It is the T.rex's massive build that makes it so frightening, so make sure its legs and body are thick and sturdy. Its head is huge in proportion to its body.

Pterodactyl

These bird-like flying reptiles look great against a dramatic sky. As your confidence grows, experiment with different wing positions. Watch real live birds to learn how wings open and fold.

Drawing tool

I drew these dinosaurs with colouring pencils. See also page 24.

Shape

Stegosaurus

The basic shape of this Stegosaurus can be adapted to many different kinds of dinosaur. With a longer neck and tail it can be turned into an Apatosaurus or Diplodocus. Shorter front legs and a larger head could make it into a Camptosaurus.

Colour

It is impossible to know the colour and patterns of these monsters. What would have been useful? Were they camouflaged to merge in with their habitat or were they highly coloured to be easily seen by others of their kind? Use your imagination. It would help to visit a zoo and study some living reptiles like lizards.

People Monsters

The starting point for all the monsters on this page is the human form, so it will help to practise drawing people in your sketchbook. Start with stick people, then build up your drawing.

Vampire

Observe

This vampire is really a man in a suit. Only his fangs give him away, although the cloak and slicked-back hair help give him a sinister air. To make the vampire look humorous, draw the fangs as big as you like.

Colour

Make the inside of the vampire's cloak red for a dramatic effect.

Here is a classic sequence of boy to monster.

Observe

Werewolves change from men to wolves at full moon. They have faces with the characteristics of both animals. Look at photographs of wolves for the nose and eyes but keep the basic arrangements of features as for a man.

Werewolf

Observe

Notice how in the early stages the changes are minimal: the hair first, then one eye and the teeth in stage 3. Even when the transformation is complete, the boy monster still wears the same clothes

Making the shadow bigger and bigger gives this sequence more drama.

Dead-people Monsters

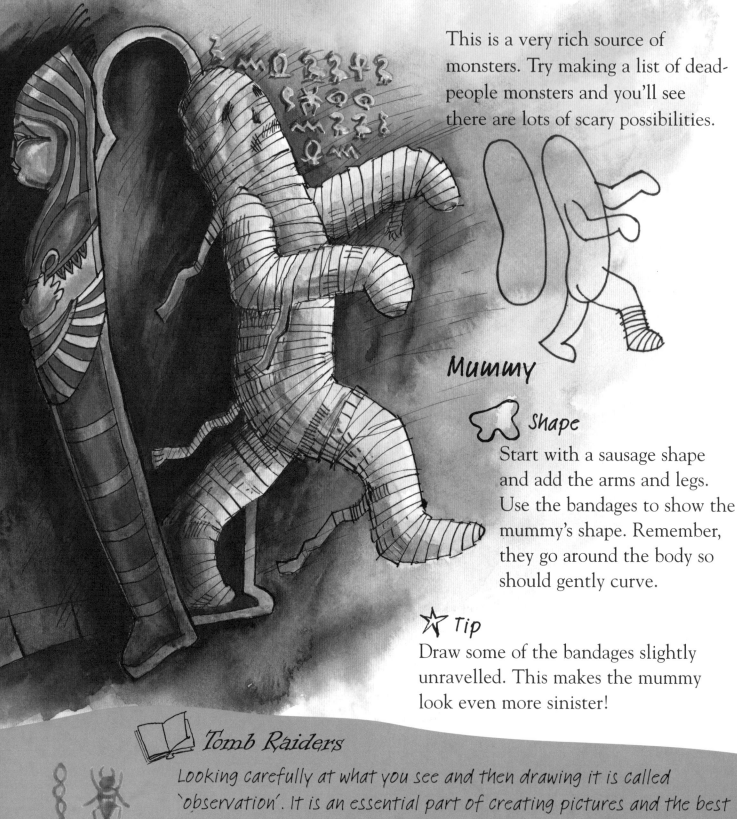

This is a very rich source of monsters. Try making a list of dead-people monsters and you'll see there are lots of scary possibilities.

Mummy

Shape
Start with a sausage shape and add the arms and legs. Use the bandages to show the mummy's shape. Remember, they go around the body so should gently curve.

☆ Tip
Draw some of the bandages slightly unravelled. This makes the mummy look even more sinister!

📖 Tomb Raiders
Looking carefully at what you see and then drawing it is called 'observation'. It is an essential part of creating pictures and the best way to improve your drawing. Try to visit a museum with your sketchbook to draw real mummies, hieroglyphs and sarcophagi. This will give you excellent reference for making pictures like this. Try and come home with a sketchbook full of notes, drawings and research.

Ghosts

These bubble-like ghosts are great fun to draw and not difficult.

Drawing tool

Use colour carefully. These ghosts are almost transparent, so you need a light, delicate touch. Watercolour or felt-pens washed over with water are ideal.

☆ Tip

Match the colour of the background in your ghost. This makes it extra-eery!

Frankenstein's Monster

Shape

This monster will look convincing if you get the proportions right. Notice the huge forehead and long arms.

☆ Tip

Frankenstein's Monster was put together out of lots of bits, so remember to show the stitching. This picture was done with collage to give the right effect.

Ghoul

Half-human Monsters

There are many monsters that are combinations of humans and different animals. To make really convincing drawings, practise drawing people and the relevant animal before trying to put them together in one creature.

Mono-print Medusa

For the drawing of Medusa opposite, I have used a process known as mono-print. It is perfect for making this scary and smudgy portrait. It is called a mono-print because unlike most ways of print-making this only makes *one* image.

You will need a piece of perspex, black oil paint and a brush or roller.

☞ **Key point**
Use oil paint because it dries slowly so the paper doesn't stick to the glass if you take a long time drawing. Be careful not to put on too much paint.

Cover the perspex with the paint. Use a brush or roller.

Lay your paper on to the painted surface and press it down lightly.

Draw Medusa on the back of the paper with a sharp pencil.

 Tips

a. Notice how the brush marks you make when painting the perspex are visible in the finished print. Use this to your advantage and 'draw' with the paint when putting it on the perspex.

b. To keep areas of the print white put pieces of paper between the painted perspex and the paper.

c. For a lighter print, press a piece of newspaper on to the painted perspex first. This will remove excess paint.

d. For dark areas rub hard with your fingers on the back of the paper.

Minotaur

In ancient Greek mythology, the Minotaur was half-bull and half-man and lived in the Labyrinth at Knossos.

Key point

When you make two different creatures into one, take one characteristic of the animal and draw it over the whole monster. So I have covered the Minotaur in the bull's fur and dotted the fish scales all over the Siren. This helps make the creature look whole.

Centaur

Half-man and half-horse.

Practise drawing horses and men first.

Siren

Not all monsters are hideous.
The Sirens were half-bird and half-mermaid and sang so beautifully from their rocky island that sailors forgot everything. They even forgot to eat and so died of hunger!

Myths and legends

If you put these creatures in their background, it helps create the right exciting and dramatic atmosphere. So read the myths and legends (Greek, Roman and Norse) and make notes in your sketchbook. Use the extra details in your drawings.

☆ Tip

Either follow these step-by-step drawings or you could make a collage using pictures of both creatures cut from magazines. It may take time to find two pictures that fit together well. Then try drawing your collage creatures.

☆ Tip
The Siren's scales should overlap like this.

Plant Monsters

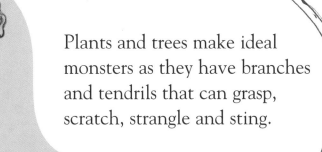

Beansprouts

1. Curl a piece of blotting paper round the inside of a glass.
2. Stuff the middle with kitchen towel.
3. Place a bean between the glass and the blotting paper. (The kitchen towel should stop the bean slipping down.)
4. Fill the glass about a quarter full of water and keep it topped-up.
5. Make a drawing each day. The bean will grow slowly at first but soon so fast that you may wish to make two drawings a day.

Plants and trees make ideal monsters as they have branches and tendrils that can grasp, scratch, strangle and sting.

Key point

Basing your drawings on real plants will make them very believable. This is a drawing of a real Venus Flytrap. The only part of it that is invented are the eyes.

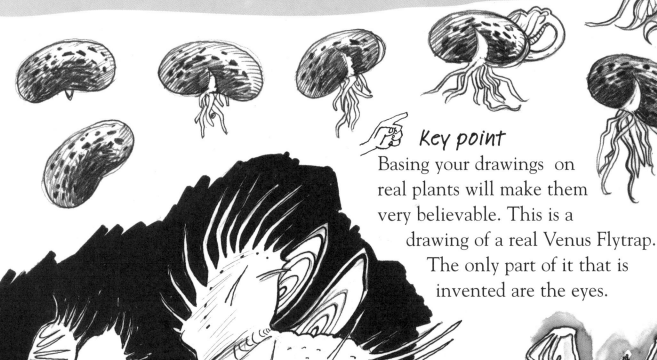

Leaf monster

Here a leaf print makes the body for this monster. Experiment with different leaves.

Key point
The best possible way to improve your drawing is to draw directly from observation (looking carefully).

Plants and trees are perfect for this as they are everywhere and they don't move.

This Triffid-like monster shoots poisonous pollen!

Tree monsters
Old and gnarled trees drawn at night need little adding to turn them into frightening monsters. Use the bark and the grain in the wood to create features. Turn branches into claw-like fingers!

Giants

Giants can be friendly and good or mean and bad. The important thing when drawing them is to make sure that they look seriously big.

☞ Key point

To emphasize the giant's size, make the background tiny. Or only show a part of him, say just an enormous pair of feet.

☆ Tip

Look at the short sleeves and trousers. If he is slightly too big for his clothes, he'll seem even bigger.

Shape

Notice how I've made this giant slightly hunched. This helps imply how tall he is, as he is always having to bend under things.

The Cyclops

These were a group of three giants who only had one eye each in the centre of their forehead. Their names were Steropes, Brontes and Arges and their job was to forge iron.

Key point

We are emphasizing the size of this cyclops because we are looking at him from an ant's-eye viewpoint. Rather like a towering skyscraper, look how he gets smaller as we look up into his staring face!

Talus

Talus was an enormous giant made of brass. He would heat himself up by lying in a fire and then rush forward to hug his enemies to his chest, so both squeezing and burning them to death!

Tip

Talus was made of brass so make your lines angular. This will help make him look hard like metal.

Colour

Add orange round Talus to give the impression that he is glowing.

Ogres

Ogres are a kind of giant with a *very* nasty character.

Smaller left eye and ear for a really wicked look.

Bushy frowning eyebrows. (Ogres are usually cross.)

Colour

Use dark, moody colours to help him look sinister.

Goggle gremlin

INKY IMP

Aargh

SPLAT spectre

Inky ogres

Splash some ink on to paper and stare at it. Can you see any shape or face? This is a really good way of creating monsters as ink blots can nearly always be turned into something. Gradually add eyes or mouths full of sharp teeth or whatever you like. You can blow the ink around by using a straw. That's a good way of creating grotesque arms and legs.

Trolls

Trolls can be big one-eyed giants or small mischievous dwarves. They can have horns, lots of arms and be covered in scales. Most have long white hair.

Observe

I've given this troll a snout-like nose and a wide grin. Although sly, trolls are often believed to be slow-witted so these characteristics help to create this impression.

Key point

As with the ogre, I've given this troll one small eye and one big eye. This helps to give him a slightly suspicious air. He looks as if he is up to no good, and WHAT is he holding behind his back?

Dragons

The word dragon comes from the Greek 'drakon' which means 'to see' and 'to watch'. When we think of dragons we usually think of them as serpents who never sleep, guarding huge hordes of treasure.

👁 Observe

This dragon, curled round his gold, is roughly egg-shaped. Gradually add details of the body, neck and head. Use curved rings around the tail and neck to make the dragon look three-dimensional.

Key point

A dragon is very like a crocodile so it will really help you to draw dragons if you look at photographs of crocodiles. Better still, go and visit a zoo to draw live crocodiles, iguanas and other large lizards.

This dragon's spiny neck and tail were based on drawings of lizards I made at London Zoo.

Dragon's hoard

You can see images of dragons everywhere: on coins, flags and coats-of-arms; as stone sculptures on castles; and as logos on packaging. Keep a drawing record in your sketchbook of as many dragons as you can find. Try preparing your sketchbook pages with patches of fiery colours to draw on. Save foil and sweet papers and stick these down to create a glittering metal surface for your dragons. Draw with a ball-point pen, wax crayon or oil pastel.

☆ Tip

You may want to cover your dragon with scales so look back at the Siren on page 13

Aliens

This really is a chance to let your imagination run wild as an alien might look like almost anything. Here is a selection of aliens to start you off but try to create your own as well.

👁 *Observe*

This *War of the Worlds-*type alien resembles both a spider and a skull and looks very scary.

☆ *Tip*

Many aliens are based on machines and robots so try to visit a science museum with your sketchbook.

📖 *Cosmic creatures*

Look through magazines and cut out scraps like eyes, animals, machinery or whatever takes your fancy. Now arrange the scraps in your sketchbook to create alien beings, the more bizarre the better. Finally make drawings from your collage creatures. You could invent a picture fact-file for them: show them eating, playing or fighting.

Shape

Start with half a sphere. Remember it is three-dimensional. Draw in the bottom section and add the skull-like eyes and nose cavity. Finally add the tripod legs to make this monster walk.

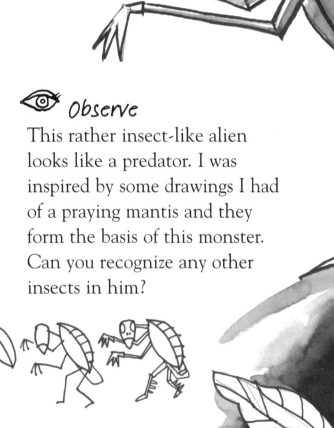

Observe

This rather insect-like alien looks like a predator. I was inspired by some drawings I had of a praying mantis and they form the basis of this monster. Can you recognize any other insects in him?

Observe

The little cluster of shapes at the end of the body hint at wings. Maybe this alien can fly!

Tip

The use of strong shadows make this picture very dramatic. Placing the frightened earthlings here creates the impression that they are already beyond help.

Many-headed Monsters

⭐ **Tip**

You could also draw all the heads separately. Cut them out and stick everything together. If you can photocopy the finished result no-one will know you did it!

Ravana

This is the evil demon king
from the Hindu epic *The
Ramayana* (see the opposite
page). He had ten heads so
drawing him is a challenge!
Try some small pictures of his
heads before attempting the
complete monster. Draw
lightly at first as you follow
the step-by-step pictures.
Try not to rub out too much.

Drawing tool

Colouring pencils are clean
and easy to use anywhere but
they are difficult to blend.

Sinister stamps

An alternative way of creating a many-headed
monster is to make a rubber stamp or card print.
The image will need to be quite simple but can be
printed endless times so it would be ideal for a
hundred-headed beast! Try creating a monster
with fifty eyes using a combination of printing and
drawing. Try out your stamps in your sketchbook.

craft knife

rubber

More Many-headed Monsters

The Lernean Hydra

A snake-like monster in Greek mythology, some say it had one hundred heads.
Others say nine but every time Hercules cut one off, two sprang up in its place!

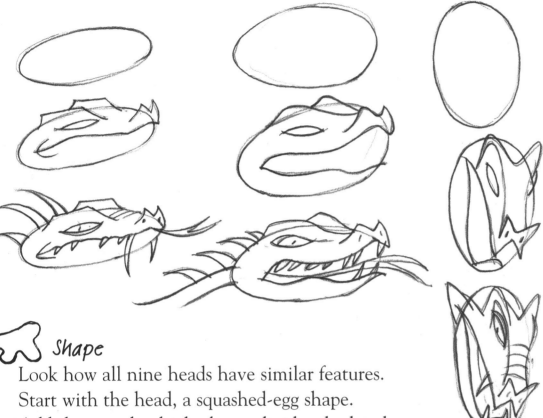

Key point
Don't be put off having a go at drawing this monster because it looks too difficult. Drawing one head will be practice for the rest.

Shape
Look how all nine heads have similar features.
Start with the head, a squashed-egg shape.
Add the mouth which almost divides the head in half, then the eyes and arching eye sockets.
The long necks get gradually thicker as they join the body.

Drawing tool
This drawing was made with a soft pencil. Notice how the shading helps us see the drawing more clearly. The dark areas show us the shape of the body and stop us getting confused by all of the hydra's heads.

The lines going round the tail and body help make this monster look solid and three-dimensional.

Sea Monsters

Krakens, Leviathans and sea serpents are monsters of the sea from classical myths. For centuries sailors have terrified us with their tales of fabulous beasts of the sea.

Here are some sea monsters for you to copy. Notice how their basic shape is similar. The neck and head rise out of the sea, as does the tail. Try creating your own sea monsters, using this as a foundation.

Fathoms-deep fish

Unbelievably, we are still discovering new species of fish that live deep, deep down at the bottom of the ocean. They are bizarre and fascinating creatures and can be seen in books or on videos. Make studies of these deep-sea fish in your sketchbook. Try drawing them in white on a black background. You can use a collection of drawings like this as a starting point for sea monsters.

Look for spouting whales and writhing sea serpents on old maps and charts. Add drawings of them to your sketchbook.

Key point

Study and draw real fish to help you achieve convincing details. You can buy fish from a fish shop or supermarket. Look at how the scales overlap and how the fins are attached. This is all part of your research and an essential part of learning to draw well.

Believe-it-or-not Monsters

Here is a double-page spread of real-life mysteries. They might really exist as there are fuzzy photographs of all of these monsters!

Abominable Snowman (or Yeti)

The Yeti lives high up in the snowy Himalayas so we might imagine it to have thick white fur.

The Loch Ness Monster

Try drawing the Loch Ness Monster in a misty, murky lake.

☆ Tip

You might find it easier to draw all of Nessie rather than just what is above the water. Then rub out the lower parts.

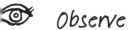 ## Observe

The Yeti and Bigfoot are quite similar as they are both ape-like monsters. Look how gorilla-like their faces are and, if you get the opportunity to draw gorillas at the zoo, this would be excellent practice.

Bigfoot

The Bigfoot has been sighted in the Canadian forests of Saskatchewan and photographs show it as a dark brown or black.

Drawing all these monsters in their natural surroundings helps persuade us that they may really exist.

Top Ten Tips

⭐ Use strong shadows to create drama.

⭐ Show part of a monster. It can sometimes be more scary than drawing all of it.

⭐ Give your monster a name. It can help trigger your imagination, e.g. Creepy Crimson Crab Eater.

⭐ The more you draw the better you will get. So practise, practise, practise.

⭐ Think where your monster lives. It may help you imagine what it looks like.

⭐ Draw from life. It will help you draw everything, not just monsters.

⭐ Always keep a sketchbook with you and draw at every available opportunity.

⭐ Practise drawing your monster from different viewpoints, and not just once.

⭐ Add written sound effects to your drawings. It can help bring them to life.

⭐ Most of all, enjoy your drawing.

GOOD LUCK!